This Land Is Your L

"California is a Garden of Eden, / A paradise to live in or see. / But believe it or not you won't find it so hot, / If you ain't got the do-re-mi."

UTAH

COLOR

Los Angeles

ROUTE 66

CALIFORNIA BORDER PATROL

OUT OF GAS

CALIFORNIA

ARIZONA

NEW M

PACIFIC OCEAN

MEXICO

NEW

"We loaded our jalopies / And piled our families in, / We rattled down that highway / To never come back again."

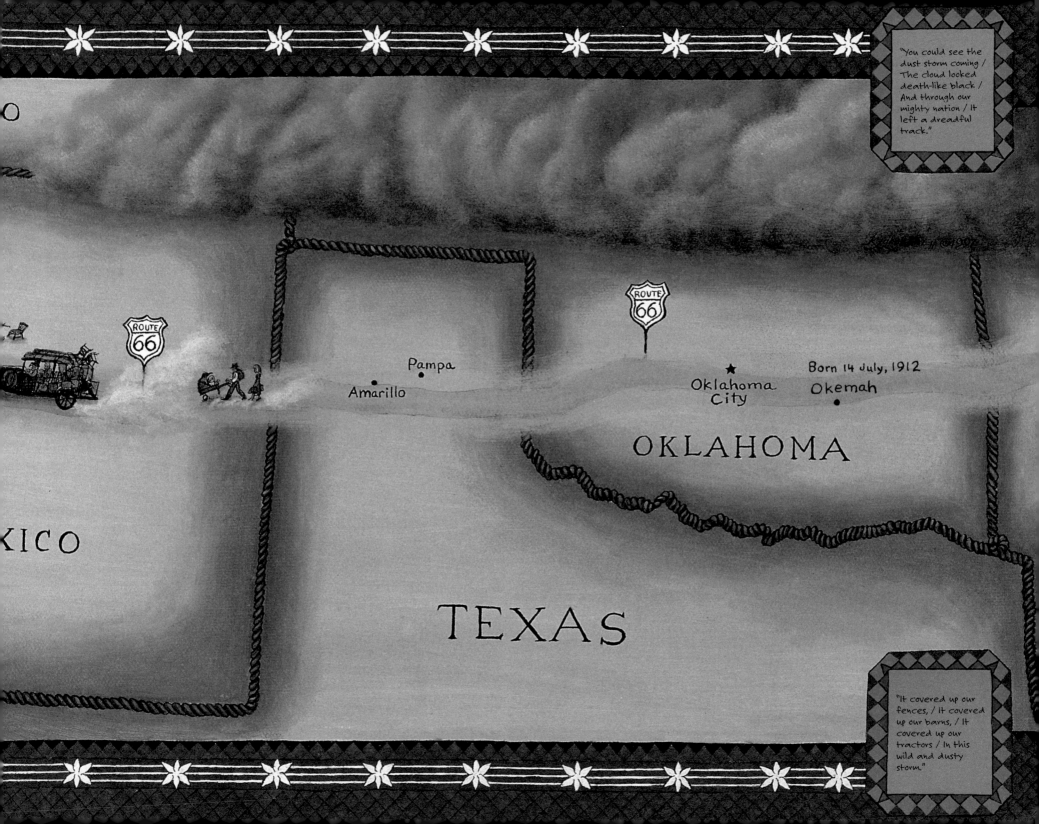

"You could see the dust storm coming / The cloud looked death-like black / And through our mighty nation / It left a dreadful track."

ROUTE 66

Pampa

Amarillo

ROUTE 66

Oklahoma City

Born 14 July, 1912

Okemah

OKLAHOMA

TEXAS

KICO

O

"It covered up our fences, / It covered up our barns, / It covered up our tractors / In this wild and dusty storm."

This Land Is

WITH A TRIBUT

Words and Music by Woody Guthrie

Your Land

BY PETE SEEGER

Paintings by Kathy Jakobsen

SCHOLASTIC INC.
New York Toronto London Auckland Sydney
Mexico City New Delhi Hong Kong

As I was walking that ribbon of highway,

I saw above me that endless skyway;

I saw below me that golden valley;

This land was made for you and me.

This land is your land, this land is my land,
From California to the New York island;

"Left wing, chicken wing, it's all the same to me."

CHILE
Woody's favorite food

"I'm goin' where the climate suits my clothes. . . . / I'm goin' where them grapes an' peaches grow."

"My land I'll defend with my life, if it be, / 'Cause my pastures of plenty must always be free."

From the redwood forest to the Gulf Stream waters,
This land was made for you and me.

"We'll all dance around and see my little seed grow."

"The sun got hot and my ground got dry. / I thought my little seed would burn and die."

"The rain it come and it washed my ground. / I thought my little seed was going to drown."

"The snow it blowed and the wind it blew; / My little seed grew and it grew and it grew."

"I stick out my little hand, / To ev'ry woman, kid and man / And I shake it up and down, / Howjido, howjido."

"On my sidewalk, on my street, / Any place that we do meet, / Then I'll shake you by your hand, / Howjido, howjido."

"I feel glad when you feel good, / You brighten up my neighborhood, / Shakin' hands with ev'rybody, / Howjido, howjido."

"When I meet a dog or cat, / I will rubby rub his back, / Shakey, shakey, shakey paw, / Howjido, howjido."

I've roamed and rambled and I followed my footsteps
To the sparkling sands of her diamond deserts;

And all around me a voice was sounding:
This land was made for you and me.

This land is your land, this land is my land,
From California to the New York island;

"Drop whatever you are doing, / Stop your work and worry, too; / Sit right down and take it easy, / Here comes Woody and Lefty Lou."

"I blowed into New York town. / I looked up and I looked down. / Everybody I seen on the streets / Was all a-running down a hole in the ground."

Hollywood Hills

HOLLYWOOD

KFVD

SUBWAY

Book #1 Songs 25¢

New York City

San Francisco

Niagara Falls

Homeless people camped out under bridge

California beach

Empire State Building

"I'm out to do the best I can / As I go ramblin' around."

Brooklyn Bridge

"I hate a song that makes you think you are just born to lose."

From the redwood forest to the Gulf Stream waters,
This land was made for you and me.

"I mined in your mines / And I gathered in your corn; / I been working, mister, / Since the day that I was born."

"Some days I'm wild / Some nights I'm tame / But no two minutes / Am I the same."

Iowa cornfield

Shrimp fishing, Gulf of Mexico

Woody's cowboy band, Pampa, Texas

California redwoods

Rodeo

Mardi Gras, New Orleans

"General Grant," giant sequoia, California

"Way down yonder in the Indian nation / I ride my pony on the reservation / In those Oklahoma hills where I was born."

"I've been having some hard traveling, / I thought you knowed . . . / I've been a-working that Pittsburgh steel."

Mississippi River

Delta Queen

Gateway Arch, St. Louis, Missouri

When the sun came shining, and I was strolling,
And the wheat fields waving and the dust clouds rolling,

As the fog was lifting a voice was chanting:
This land was made for you and me.

This land is your land, this land is my land,
From California to the New York island;

"It's a mighty hard row that my poor hands have hoed; / My poor feet have traveled a hot dusty road."

'Wherever men are fightin' for their rights, / That's where I'm gonna be, Ma, / That's where I'm gonna be."

Migrant farmworkers

Los Angeles City Hall

Okemah, Oklahoma

THE GRAPES OF WRATH   CRYSTAL

Woody singing at a migrant camp

Dust Bowl refugees

Garment workers

Water tower, Chicago

"So long, it's been good to know ye, / This dusty old dust is a getting my home, / And I've got to be drifting along."

Hobo train

"Oh you can't scare me, / I'm sticking to the union. / I'm sticking to the union / till the day I die."

From the redwood forest to the Gulf Stream waters,
This land was made for you and me.

"Roll on, Columbia, roll on. / Your power is turning our darkness to dawn, / So, roll on, Columbia, roll on!"

"This train is bound for glory, this train. / This train is bound for glory. / Don't carry nothing but the righteous and the holy."

Grand Coulee Dam construction

Northern train ride

Columbia River, Crown Point, Oregon

Picking peaches

"Old Faithful," Yellowstone National Park

Wawona tunnel tree, Yosemite National Park

Oil well

"I caught myself a ride off down a Texas freight train. / Name on the boxcar was the Santy Fee."

Dining car train

"I've worked in your orchards of peaches and prunes . . . / On the edge of your city you've seen us and then, / We come with the dust and we go with the wind."

As I went walking, I saw a sign there,
And on the sign it said "No Trespassing."

No Trespassing
Keep Off!

But on the other side it didn't say nothing;
That side was made for you and me.

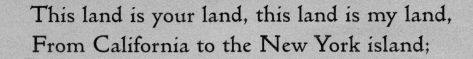

This land is your land, this land is my land,
From California to the New York island;

Diamond Head and Waikiki Beach, Honolulu

Coney Island Amusement Park

Steeplechase
The Funny Pla

CYCLO

Chinese Theater, Hollywood

Grand Canyon

Coney Island beach

FOR GLORY

BOUND FOR GLORY

Upper and Lower Yosemite Falls

Washington Monument

Crazy Horse Memorial, South Dakota

Mount Rushmore, South Dakota

Stone Mountain Memorial, Georgia

From the redwood forest to the Gulf Stream waters,
This land was made for you and me.

"Songs come to me best when walking down the road."

"The people are building a peaceful world, and when the job is done, / That'll be the biggest thing that man has ever done."

Firestone Farm, Greenfield Village, Michigan

Portland Head Light Station, Maine

Woody on the road

Mesa Verde, Colorado

Seattle Space Needle

Space Shuttle launch, Florida

Oak Alley, Vacherie, Louisiana

"So go the new road and see the new things — feel the new way and breathe the new air."

"My daddy rides that ship in the sky. / Mama's not afraid and neither am I."

Brooks Range, Alaska

In the shadow of the steeple I saw my people;
By the relief office I seen my people;

As they stood there hungry, I stood there asking,
Is this land made for you and me?

This land is your land, this land is my land,
From California to the New York island;

From the redwood forest to the Gulf Stream waters,
This land was made for you and me.

"Dancie dance dance / singy sing sing / grow grow grow / biggy big big."

"Dance around and around and around and around, / Dance around and around and around."

Pete Seeger singing at the Clearwater Festival

CLEARWATER

Marjorie Guthrie's dance class

Boston Pops performing "This Land" at Fourth of July celebration

Watts Towers, Los Angeles

Totem pole, Ketchikan, Alaska

"All any kind of music is good for anyway is to make you and me know each other a little better."

"You hear your own music inside your own self."

"This world is your world and my world. Take it easy, but take it."

Woody Guthrie and friends singing his songs, 1935–1967
Left to right: Woody Guthrie, Leadbelly, Lefty Lou, Cisco Houston, Will Geer, Tom Paxton, Ramblin' Jack Elliott, Lee Hays, Ronnie Gilbert, Pete Seeger, Fred Hellerman, Joan Baez, Arlo Guthrie, Phil Ochs, Odetta, Bob Dylan, Judy Collins, Richie Havens, Peter Yarrow, Mary Travers, Paul Stookey. Seated: Sonny Terry, Brownie McGhee

"Some will rob you with a six-gun, / And some with a fountain pen."

New York, 1940

"All you can write is what you see."

Woody Guthrie tribute concert, Rock and Roll Hall of Fame, Cleveland 1996
Row 1 (left to right): Paul Metza, Dave Pirner, Emily Saliers, Amy Ray, Dan Bern, David Lutken, James Stein, Mimi Bessette, Lisa Asher, Neil Woodward
Row 2 (left to right): Alejandro Escovedo, David Perales, John Wesley Harding, Jimmy LaFave, Jimmie Dale Gilmore, Syd Straw, Ani DiFranco, Ramblin' Jack Elliott, Pete Seeger, Bruce Springsteen, Arlo Guthrie, Country Joe McDonald, Nora Guthrie, Anna Guthrie Rotante, Billy Bragg, Joe Ely, Jorma Kaukonen, Tim Robbins, Harold Leventhal

"I have room for one more friend and he is Everyman."

Nobody living can ever stop me,
As I go walking that freedom highway;

Nobody living can ever make me turn back;
This land was made for you and me.

This land is your land, this land is my land,
From California to the New York island;

A Tribute to
WOODY GUTHRIE

Woody and Pete Seeger at one of the many concerts they played together

Courtesy of the Woody Guthrie Archives

"A FOLK SONG IS WHAT'S WRONG AND HOW TO FIX IT OR IT COULD BE WHO'S HUNGRY AND WHERE THEIR MOUTH IS OR WHO'S OUT OF WORK AND WHERE THE JOB IS OR WHO'S BROKE AND WHERE THE MONEY IS OR WHO'S CARRYING A GUN AND WHERE THE PEACE IS."
— WOODY GUTHRIE

I first heard "This Land Is Your Land" on the Folkways recording, 1949. My first reaction was "It's a nice idea, but the tune is too simple. This song is one of Woody's lesser efforts."

That shows how wrong you can be. Over the years I've realized that it's easy to get complicated. But Woody had a genius for simplicity. This song now has reached hundreds of millions of people.

Maybe billions of people.

The song was never on the Top 40, but it got into schools and summer camps. It went from one guitar picker to another. I now get audiences singing every verse without needing any songbooks, because I call out the words to them line by line without losing the rhythm.

When some high voices can add harmony, like two notes above the melody, then we get hope for the future of the human race.

Woody wrote the song in the windy, icy February of 19 and 40, when he hitchhiked from Los Angeles to New York City. The original fourth line of each verse then was "God blessed America for me." (Irving Berlin's famous song, sung by Kate Smith, was on all the jukeboxes in the roadside diners at that time.)

I never heard Woody sing it till 1949, when he recorded it for the tiny Folkways Recording Company with the fourth line we all know now.

He wrote thousands of songs. The 1949 recording of "This Land," and later the school songbooks, omitted some of the best verses. Nowadays Arlo Guthrie and I and many others make sure to include them. Because it's important to remember that if the sign says "No Trespassing" on one side, on the other side "It didn't say nothing. That side was made for you and me."

Somewhere Woody is grinning and saying to us all, "Take it easy, but take it!"

— PETE SEEGER. 1998

Woody as a baby with his sister, Clara

WOODY GUTHRIE was born on July 14, 1912, in the dusty little town of Okemah, Oklahoma. Charley and Nora Guthrie named their son Woodrow Wilson, but everybody called him "plain old Woody."

When Woody was six, his family started having some hard luck. Their new house burned down, and a few years later, Woody's sister died in a fire. His mother got sick and had to live in a hospital.

When Woody was seventeen, he moved to Texas. In flat, windy Pampa, he found an old guitar and learned to play. He liked to sing ballads — long songs that tell a story. He formed a band with some friends and started writing songs about his experiences and the folks he met along the way.

In 1929, people everywhere faced hard times. They called this period the Great Depression. In Texas, it stopped raining. Fierce winds piled dust over the land. The farms around Pampa "dried up and blowed away." Someone said it looked like a big dust bowl. And it did.

Lots of folks in that Dust Bowl packed up and headed for California, looking for jobs and new homes. Woody headed west, too, hitching rides and hopping freight trains when he could. California was filling up with people from Oklahoma, Texas, and other states. These travelers were called migrants or "Okies."

The migrants ended up in crowded camps. Their "homes" were tents and small rooms pieced together from scraps. And there weren't enough jobs to go around.

The Guthrie family on their porch in Okemah

Woody's band in Pampa, Texas. He is the first "cowboy" on the left.

"MY EYES HAS BEEN MY CAMERA TAKING PICTURES OF THE WORLD AND MY SONGS HAS BEEN MESSAGES THAT I TRIED TO SCATTER ACROSS THE BACK SIDES AND ALONG THE STEPS OF THE FIRE ESCAPES AND ON THE WINDOWSILLS AND THROUGH THE DARK HALLS."

One of many families on the road to California

> "A SONG DON'T HAVE TO BE AS OLD AS THE HILLS TO BE GOOD, TRUE, OR HONEST. SONGS THAT TELL THE TRUE BATTLE OF OUR PEOPLE TO GET BETTER AND BETTER CONDITIONS EVERYWHERE ARE AS GOOD HOT OR COLD, NEW OR OLD, JUST SO'S THEY'RE HONEST."

Woody entertains some migrant workers.

> "LOTS OF SONGS I MAKE UP WHEN I'M LAUGHING AND CELEBRATING MAKE FOLKS CRY, AND SONGS I MAKE UP WHEN I'M FEELING DOWN AND OUT MAKE PEOPLE LAUGH. THESE TWO UPSIDE-DOWN FEELINGS HAS GOT TO BE IN ANY SONG TO MAKE IT TAKE A HOLD AND LAST."

Courtesy of the Woody Guthrie Archives

IN CALIFORNIA, Woody got a job singing on the radio. His show was popular in the migrant camps. After visiting the camps himself, Woody started writing songs about the migrants—their hard luck and their courage.

In 1940, when he was twenty-eight, Woody went to New York City. He sang for factory workers trying to get better working conditions and higher pay. He sang on street corners with new friends like Pete Seeger and Leadbelly. He began to record his songs, including a new one called "This Land Is Your Land." He also wrote a book about his life titled *Bound for Glory*.

When World War II broke out, Woody sailed to Europe with the merchant marine on large ships carrying supplies and soldiers. After the war, he came home and wrote children's songs for his little daughter Cathy and her friends. Kids were some of Woody's favorite audiences.

In 1952, Woody learned he had Huntington's disease. He was forty years old. He wrote, played his guitar, and visited friends and family a few more years, but finally went to live in a hospital.

By the time he died, in 1967, Woody had written more than one thousand songs, including the classics "Deportee," "Pastures of Plenty," and "Roll On, Columbia;" two novels based on his life; and hundreds of stories. Because he always spoke out for people of all colors and races, especially the poor, he inspired many musicians to do the same.

"Stick up for what you know is right," Woody wrote. "This land was made for you and me."

Eric Schaal, *Life Magazine* © Time Inc.

Woody picks guitar for some young fans.

Stephen Deutsch, Chicago Historical Society. Neg. 38902

Woody with his good friend Leadbelly

This Land Is Your Land

Words and Music by Woody Guthrie

As I was walking that ribbon of highway,
I saw above me that endless skyway;
I saw below me that golden valley;
This land was made for you and me.

[Chorus]

I've roamed and rambled and I followed my footsteps
To the sparkling sands of her diamond deserts;
And all around me a voice was sounding:
This land was made for you and me.

[Chorus]

When the sun came shining, and I was strolling,
And the wheat fields waving and the dust clouds rolling,
As the fog was lifting a voice was chanting:
This land was made for you and me.

[Chorus]

As I went walking, I saw a sign there,
And on the sign it said "No Trespassing."
But on the other side it didn't say nothing;
That side was made for you and me.

[Chorus]

In the shadow of the steeple I saw my people;
By the relief office I seen my people;
As they stood there hungry, I stood there asking,
Is this land made for you and me?

[Chorus]

Nobody living can ever stop me,
As I go walking that freedom highway;
Nobody living can ever make me turn back;
This land was made for you and me.

Note: In the Canadian version, the chorus lyrics "From California...to the Gulf Stream waters" are replaced by "From Bonavista to Vancouver Island; / From the Arctic Circle to the Great Lake waters." And in the second verse, the lyrics "To the sparkling sands of her diamond deserts" are replaced by "To the fir-clad forests of our mighty mountains." These words were written by the Travellers, a Canadian folk group.

To my kids, Anna and Cole—
Grandpa loves you! —Nora Guthrie

To my father, Frank W. J.
Love you, Pop! —Kathy Jakobsen

ISBN 0-439-13225-8

The paintings for this book were done in oil on canvas. The painted borders were inspired by notch carvings found in traditional "tramp art" – boxes, picture frames, and mirror frames crafted by tramps, hoboes, miners, and lumberjacks in the early to mid-1900s. The artist researched Woody Guthrie's life extensively, and the illustrations feature people and places that were important in his life and travels.

For more information about Woody Guthrie, please contact the Woody Guthrie Archives, at 250 West 57th Street, Suite 1218, New York, NY 10107.

"California is a Garden of Eden, / A paradise to live in or see. / But believe it or not you won't find it so hot, / If you ain't got the do-re-mi."

UTAH

COLORA

ROUTE 66

CALIFORNIA BORDER PATROL

Los Angeles

OUT OF GAS

CALIFORNIA

ARIZONA

NEW M

PACIFIC OCEAN

MEXICO

"We loaded our jalopies / And piled our families in, / We rattled down that highway / To never come back again."

"You could see the dust storm coming / The cloud looked death-like black / And through our mighty nation / It left a dreadful track."

O

ROUTE 66

ROUTE 66

Pampa

Amarillo

Oklahoma City

Born 14 July, 1912
Okemah

OKLAHOMA

XICO

TEXAS

"It covered up our fences, / It covered up our barns, / It covered up our tractors / In this wild and dusty storm."